ENDINGS?

hopeful - depressing - melancholies
about anything
i think i can't have.

think again.

by anand
with additional illustrations
by bernarda saldo
and friends

FUTURA HOUSE

Library of Congress Cataloging-in-Publication Data
Stratton, Mary-Margaret (anand sahaja)
Endings?

Summary: "hopeful - depressing - melancholies about anything i think i can't have. think again. Writings about that living hell, that limbo, those lost long years, that we sometimes call love. Loss is sometimes real. Sometimes not. You never know if that door closed for a reason?" – Provided by the publisher.

ISBN-13: 978-0-9998749-4-3
ISBN-10: 0-9998749-4-2

1. Literature and Fiction >

Published by Futura House
2620 South Maryland Parkway #345
Las Vegas, NV 89109
Printed in the United States of America
www.futurahouse.com

Book Design and Images by MM Stratton (megorama.com) using American Typewriter

table of contents

dedication

to the muses of charles bukowski
and sylvia plath.
to jeanne farrens.
and to mr. nobody for inspiration.

fore-words

Writings about that living hell,
that limbo, those lost long years,
that we sometimes call love.

Loss is sometimes real.
Sometimes not.
You never know if that door closed
for a reason?

pane

we were lying on the bed
and he threw something
towards my bookcase
(his keys I think)
and smashed the pane of glass.
he wasn't too regretful either.
said he would fix it
but never did.

years later
i haven't repaired it
i don't know if i'm still waiting for him
or maybe
i just don't want to mend
the pain of
the shattered past.

pass the pills

i cannot live
with myself
when
you cannot live
with yourself
so obviously
we cannot live
with each other,
but
i cannot live
without you

somebody
pass the pills

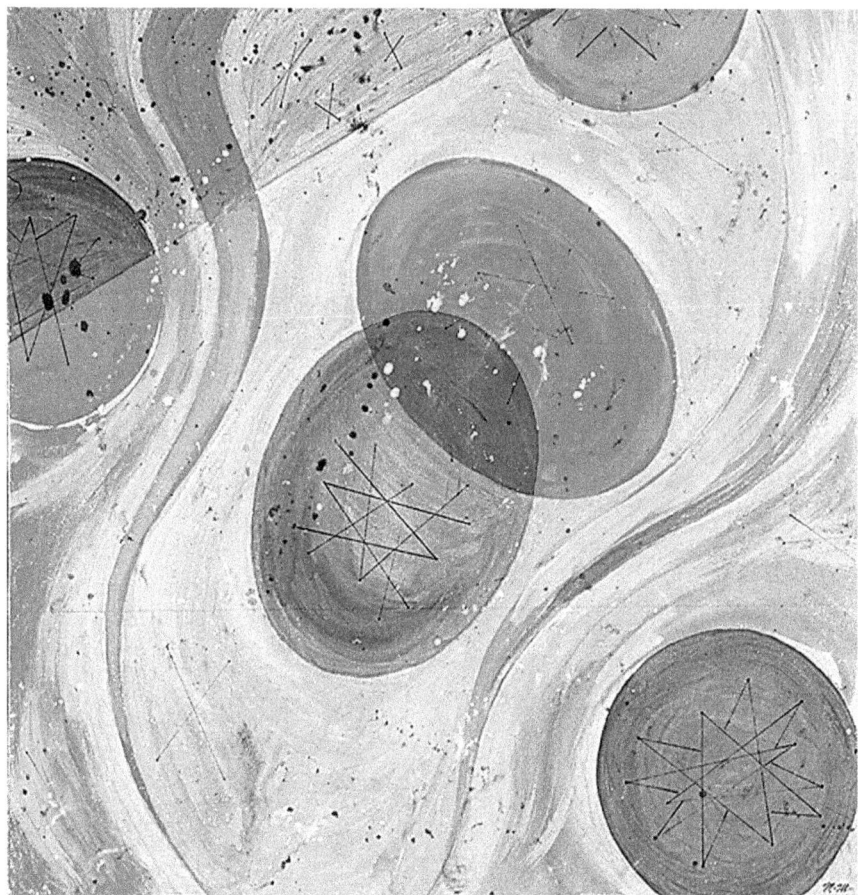

another time

in another time
we were two hands
of the same motion
in perfect time

now we go round and round
somehow always passing each other by
countless revolutions later
i'm still ready to try
another time.

the appendix
is my friend

the slings and arrows of outrageous misfortune
have left me alone at last

and the depression and ensuing insomnia
lead me to abstain from abstinence

my addiction launches forth
spiraling downward and backwards

to the foregone conclusion and inevitable end
as the pain in my abdomen reminds me

the pharma matrix is based on supply
and demand.
if you can't beat 'em join 'em.

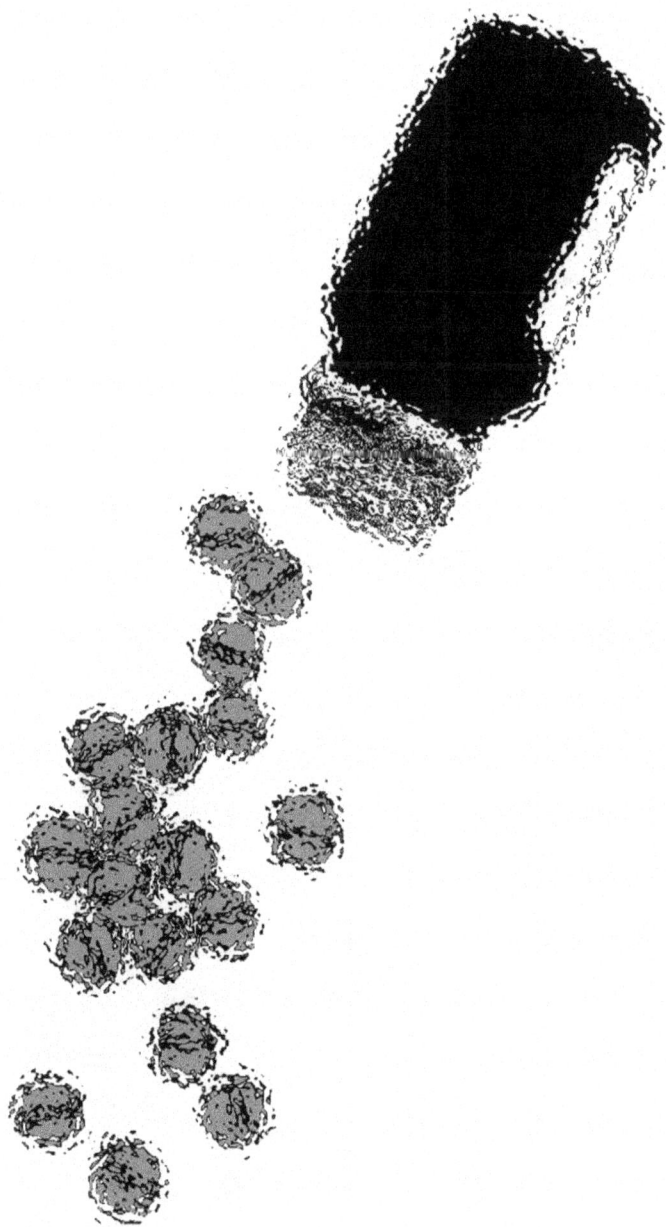

cricket's content

windows wide
to drink in the cool
crickets content
chirpit. chirpit. chirpit.
they sing so happy & optimistic
can't they leave some

air
or
some
space
peace for the distressed.

how many of them are there anyway?

damn crickets

blue boy

little boy blue
curly blond hair
grew up to find himself
not so adorable.
shot himself last night
now he's a redhead.

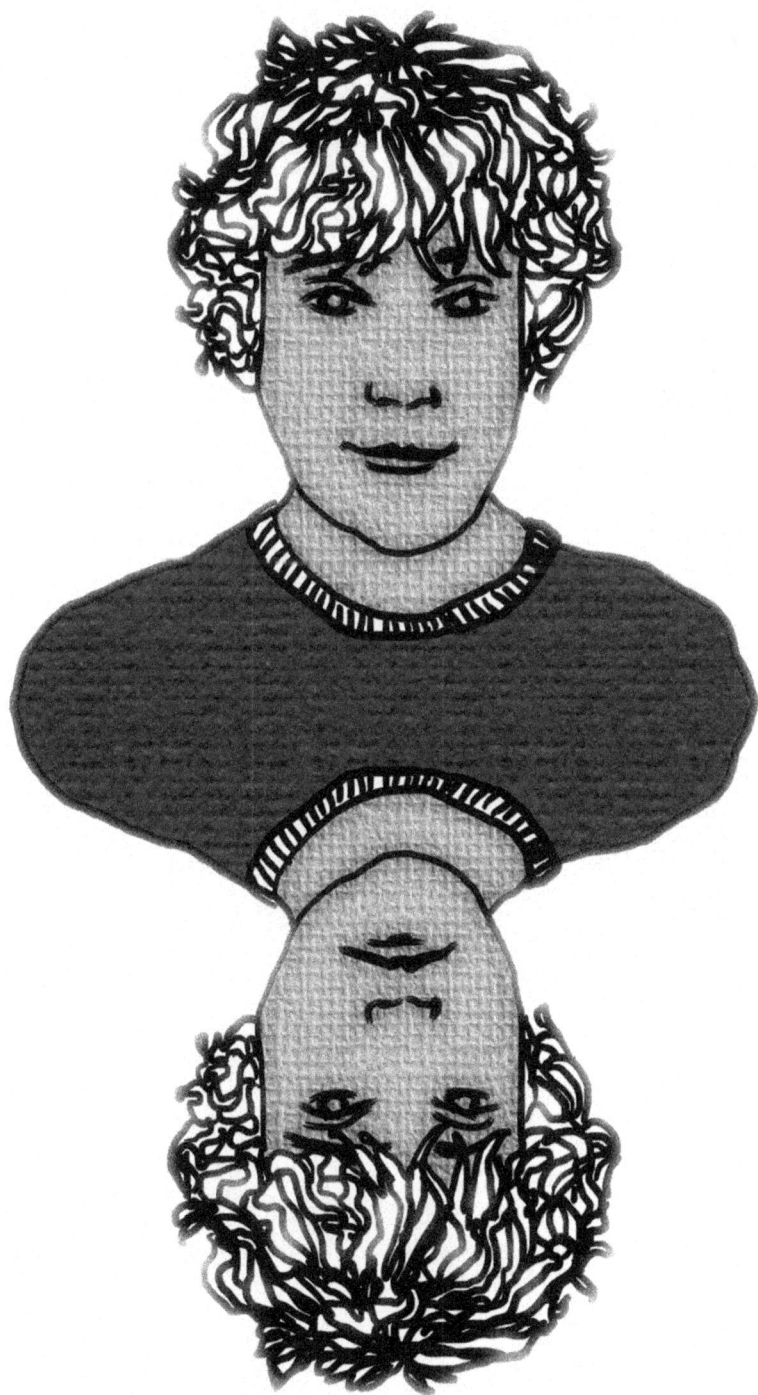

I 2

strange
2 think of U
with another.
I 2
have done the same
but always
came back 2U

I need some thing
more than leverage
2 wrench U
from my gut.

won't change the fact
that U R in bed
with a stranger
2 night

Buddies

Unrequited Sonnet

It was my sole desire
to have you for my own,
methinks you're a liar
with a heart made of stone.
If i could just seduce you
and get you to my place,
I'd ply you with a brew
to tell me to my face
of the feelings you feel.
And then I'd find out why
you made such a big deal
of love that you deny.
When that day comes and I corner you,
I'll have my revenge and we will be through!

reaping in a grim cocktail

i romance death
every day i drink
in the bottom of an amber glass
lies my hooded sickle laden friend

i love to live
but i know i will leave
the earth someday
someway

so in the meantime i seek
to know blissful oblivion
of sleepless slumber
resting in peace
at the bottom of my amber glass

such a pretty way to go

over

over and over
I tell myself
it's over
done finished completed
ended
the fat lady sang.

but
when and what she sang
just reminded me
i'm not over you.

want for wanting

I do not want vengeance.
Karma
has her own way of
righting wrongs.
I do not seek revenge.
No more slashed tires in the dark
and sabotaged stages.
No, I do not want violence.

I seek a peaceful solution
Because I am calm enough
now to accept
what has not been
and what will not be.

I only want
for wanting.

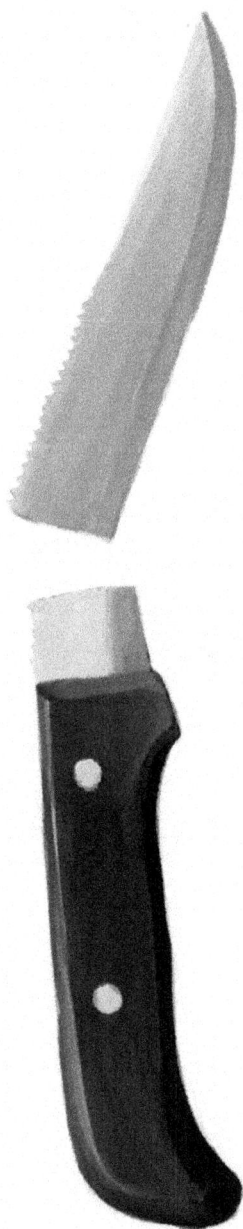

Pissed

At Lenny's party
I left early because
the beers in the fridge
disappeared too early.
So I fell over the couch
and hugged
Jerry, Chris, Tom, etc. goodbye.
Outside
Jeff was at the back side of his car
feeding the flowers.
I turned the headlights on and left.
He laughed on the phone the next day
proudly describing how drunk he was last night
apparently all the beer
didn't just disappear.

spent

the seconds click on
whittling away
at what's left
of my life.

no sooner do
i think i have
a decent paycheck
it's spent
before it arrives.

my seconds
are spent, too.
start to add
life up
and the time
doesn't amount to much.
done before it's begun.

another 30 seconds less now.

He's Not Listening

"My fingernails hurt,"
she said as she reached back
and picked up a pencil.
"I'll draw hangnails
chewed to the quick
because of you, you know."
At this she thoughtfully gazed
at the sketchbook on her lap.
"Why don't they
make these pre-drawn."
And dug her teeth into the wood.

He humph'd in agreement
50 or so miles down the road.

She replied: "I wish I were a man.
Then the cuts and scars of my life
wouldn't be so repulsive.
They'd simply reveal my character."

you left

I went out of my mind
when you left,
you left, you left, you left.
and now I am praying for yours.

Don't destroy your mind
while you're away,
'cause if you're ever back,
back, back, back, back,
I want all the mental stimulation
to be omnipresent.

When you see me again
It will be God's punch
to knock you back, back, back
to your senses.
And you will wonder just
how far out of your mind you were
to leave.

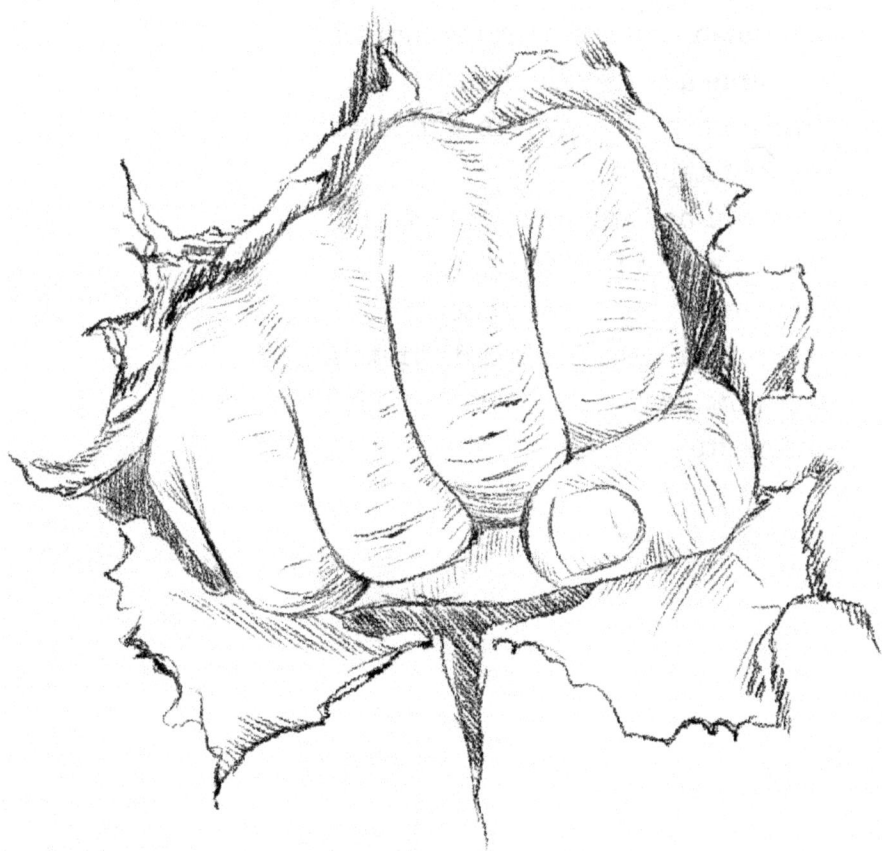

order

once i was a free spirit
until i met order.
his conformity intrigued me
and brought me into the dark of reality.
for once i was a hopeful romantic,
i became a hopeless one.
i would try to tease him and lighten
his footsteps and heart,
but each had its own set rhythm.
soon my soul flutterings
became almost non-existent,
and my dancing slowed down to a beat,
and now i work only with words
and write on lines.

counting on
the rhythms of
the sea

(and getting splashed in the face)

your speech
uneven as the tide we ride upon
halting and dropping
sometimes you're there
and sometimes you're not
the ride is precarious
and leaves me too exposed

within the bow of your arms
i turn to the sea
to find an ocean
full of holes.

paper

I've actually seen
the fibers it takes
to make paper.
If it hadn't been for you
I would have never noticed.

It is the sigh of your
boredom and constancy
that makes me listen
and search out
and scrutinize
other life affirming facets
like the paper in my hand
bond bland and flat
like you
with minimal texture
and lack of color.

and yet there is so much
i could create with you
if you would allow the exposure,
and if
I don't dry up soon.

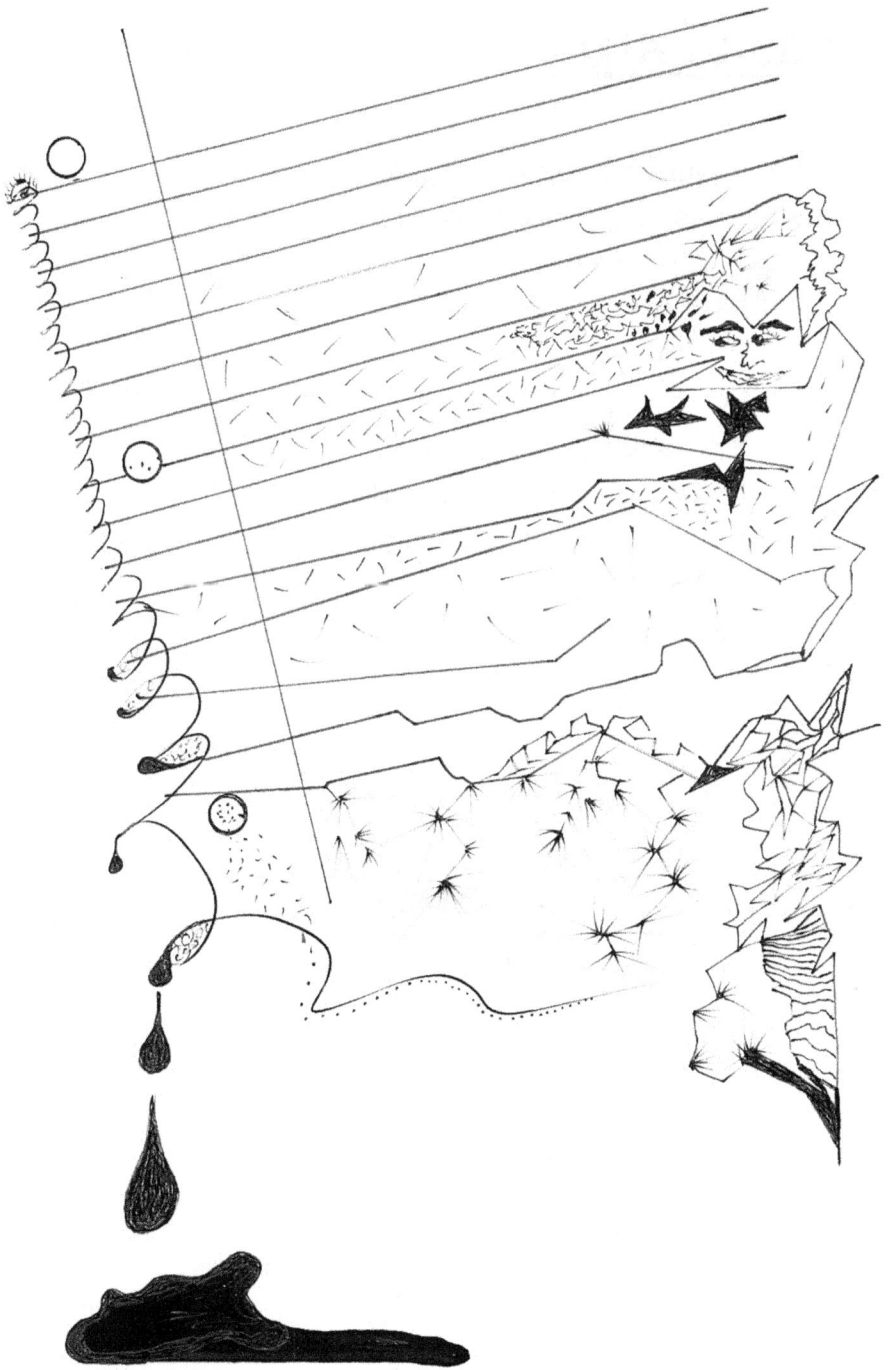

Ode to Billy

Shall I compare you to summer skies
the blue as bright as the blue in your eyes:
a broad expanse before me
in which i see eternity.

Shall I compare you to a winter night
a black crystal reflecting light;
an inscrutable shard of the day
cold and clear and so far away.

egomaniac

i met an egomaniac
he seemed to have it all.
looks
money
popularity
passable personality
but there is one major thing he'll never have.

me.

hungry

being broken
is like
fuck fuck fuck
and everything else
I can think of.
rocking myself to sleep
just to make up for
lost hugs and
empty embraces.
searching every mouth
for the one that will
fill
the hollow.

my stomach
gets upset with me
for wanting
to feed one hole,
but not
the other.

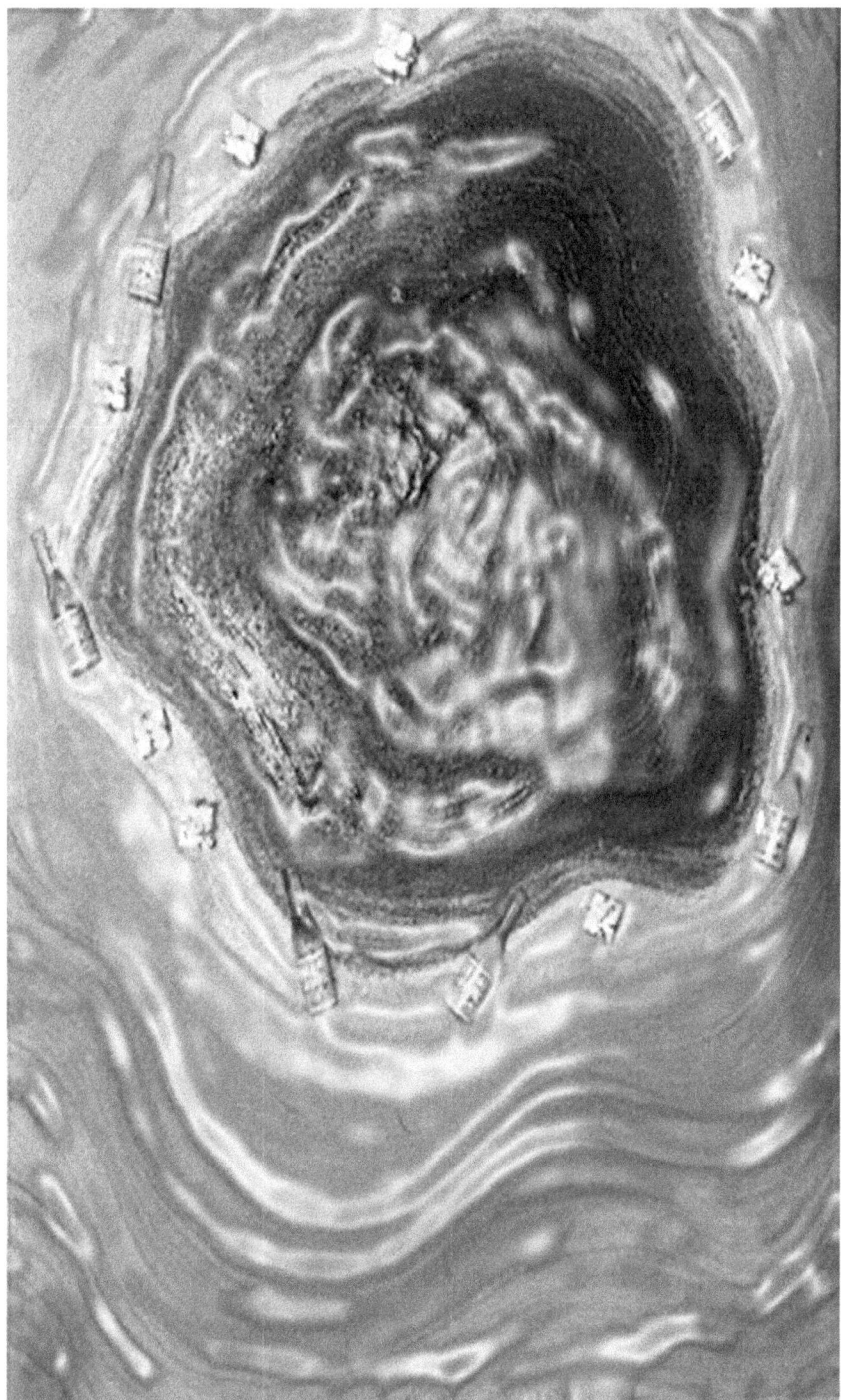

My Plan

Accept my faults,
but do not dwell on them.
For the more time you give them,
the more important they become
and the less time
you'll have to see the rest of me.

Don't take too long
to sweep me up in your arms.
And don't give me time
to re-examine your faults
or review the situation,
because I've always planned on love
to be impetuous and spontaneous.

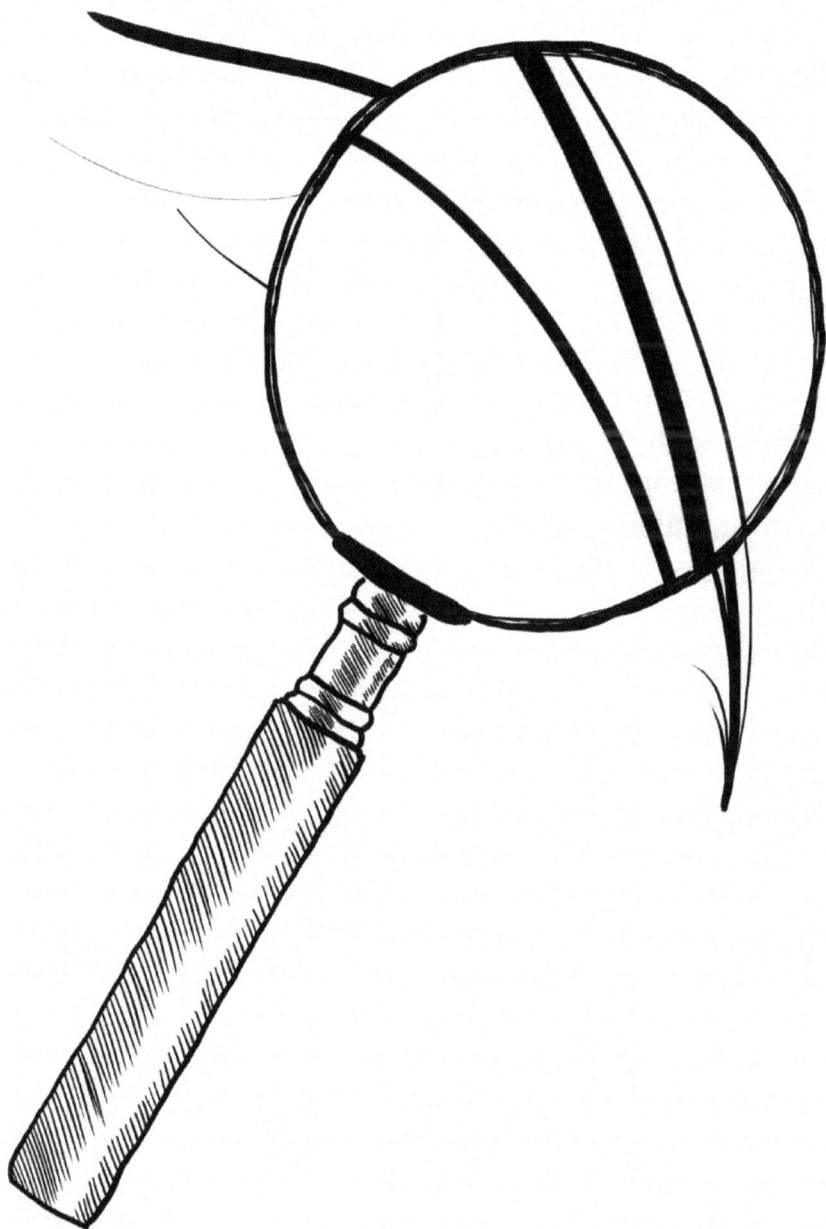

sandy castles

well worn memories
like sandy castles
on the shore

eroding with the wind
washed up with
the saltwater tide
and time
rounding away
softening the edges
before sweeping them away
with one final
goodbye wave

Wave Goodbye

Once we were
tuned in,
on the same wavelength.
His broadcast
was the best I'd heard.
I learned by listening
and he was glad to have
a live audience.
His voice was music
that played around in my head,
swept me off my feet

But he changed the frequency
blamed me for not being receptive.
I didn't know what station to turn to.
So I called on the phone,
but there were no more requests
and I was left listening
to dead air space.

caged

we are two animals
trapped in a cage
of self denial
and self deprival
you sit in acceptance
and watch me pace

CAUGHT

night lights

civilization lights far
distant like the star lights
in a winter sky
without tangible life

friends

a knock in the dark
in the middle of night
a talk in the dark
by dim candlelight
an exchange of thoughts
about lovers and why
we don't kiss goodnight
just handshake goodbye

Finding Fault at a Fork in our Relationship

the definition of repression:
eating French fries
with friends
at four AM
with a fork.

at such an hour
it is a mandatory standard
to eat French fries
with your fingers.

American Empire Will Fall

"eternal vigilance is the price of liberty"
Thomas Jefferson

Walter had an idea
He scribbled down on a page,
Gave it a personal name
And plenty of time to age.
Who can save us now, that
Time and the Left have undone?
No razor stubble and a fifties flair
Virtual battles can never be won.

Alfred had an idea
That one murder was enough
Now even serial killers
Don't even seem that tough.
Disposable is life, oh,
How can we get much further?
No band of gypsies and a sixties cry
We're desensitized, yet full of terror.

The world's an overload of stimuli
Too many people and not enough room.
The god of the underworld is chillin' in Denver.
He's hanging out in a plutonium tomb.
Whatever becomes of us all,
The American Empire will fall.

Cloudburst

The garden was dry
in need of rain yesterday.
He had not come home
after leaving the night before.
The screen door clattered as he slammed it.
The dusty Chevy truck sputtered to a start
and hard dirt flew from the tires
as he sped away
past the low broken chain link
and stingy weeds

The air was thick and damp
before the clouds burst
into the stillness.

That was last night,
but my pillow is still damp.
He said this time
I wouldn't be his clinging vine
and shook me off.

The ground is left wet,
But I am wrung out to dry.

inadvertently

people ask how
could he be such a fool
to leave me?

and he was
a fool

but within wisdom.

had he not left
I may not
have become
the woman
he so
foolishly left.

love is not lovely

love is
not always lovely
and 'beautiful music'
is rarely
beautiful

certainly uncertain

one moment a monument
fixed in your memory
I stood unshaken

now you'd rather stay home
without the reminder
of the past

and I am one
you rarely visit

Shower

warm rivulets
run through my hair
finding their way
over the curves
of my body.
i live in a liquid world.
my cupped hands overflow
with the warm water.
i cannot breath.

you felt your way
quickly to my skin
and covered me and
tried to control me,
but i will not hold you
in upturned palms.
i will let you slide
past my grasp
to depart
down the drain
out of my life

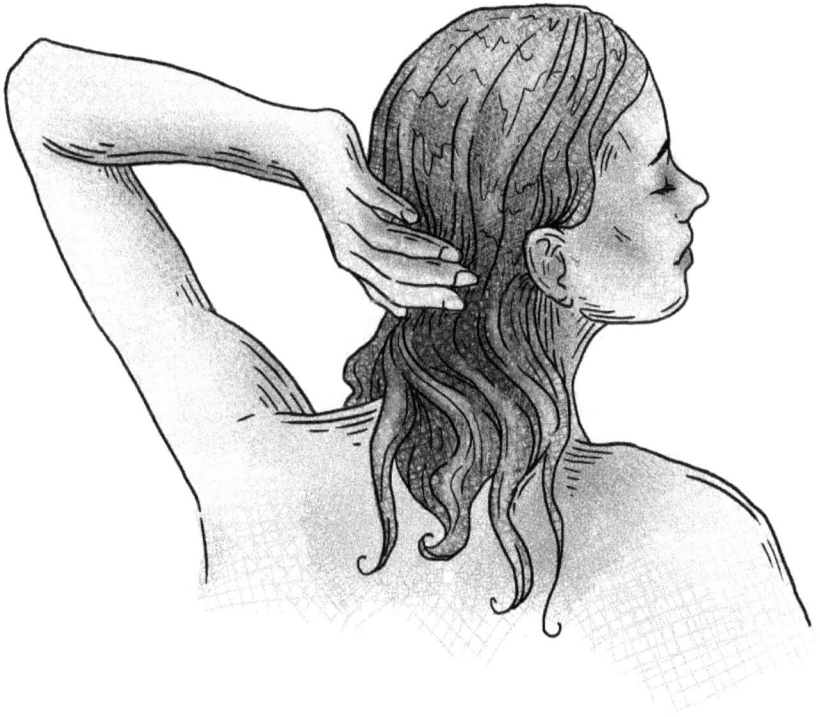

Goddamn God

Goddamn God
The one who told the Hebrews
to wipe out civilizations
and said incest was OK
to carry on the family line.

Goddamn God
who let man be free
to fuck over his fellow man
(or woman)
and allows evil
to continue its course.

Goddamn God
who preached love
but never did anything
to insure its endurance.

sole support

I stored your love notes away
in an old green shoe box.

A pile of letters held
by ribbons and cardboard
are there to support me,
when regular shoes
aren't enough.

Without

Without
a will
to live.

the planet
too small,
the people
too similar,
the space
too same,

pointless.

there is no
logical reason
to continue
within
such limits.

but is there
really anything
worthwhile

without.

by and bye

by and by
i am saying
good-bye.

there are still
little things
that fishhook
into my heart,
but i'm a
bigger fish
thrown back into
a wider ocean
so I must survive
and swim
by.

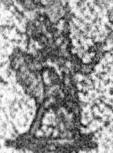

A Writer's Question

Why is it
when violence
has vanished
there is
no poetry
to write?

To dream
perchance of writing.
aye, there's the rub.
Is it better to
lose oneself
in the illusion
of contentment,
or better still
to find contentment
and surrender to a safe cove
away from a sea
of troubles?

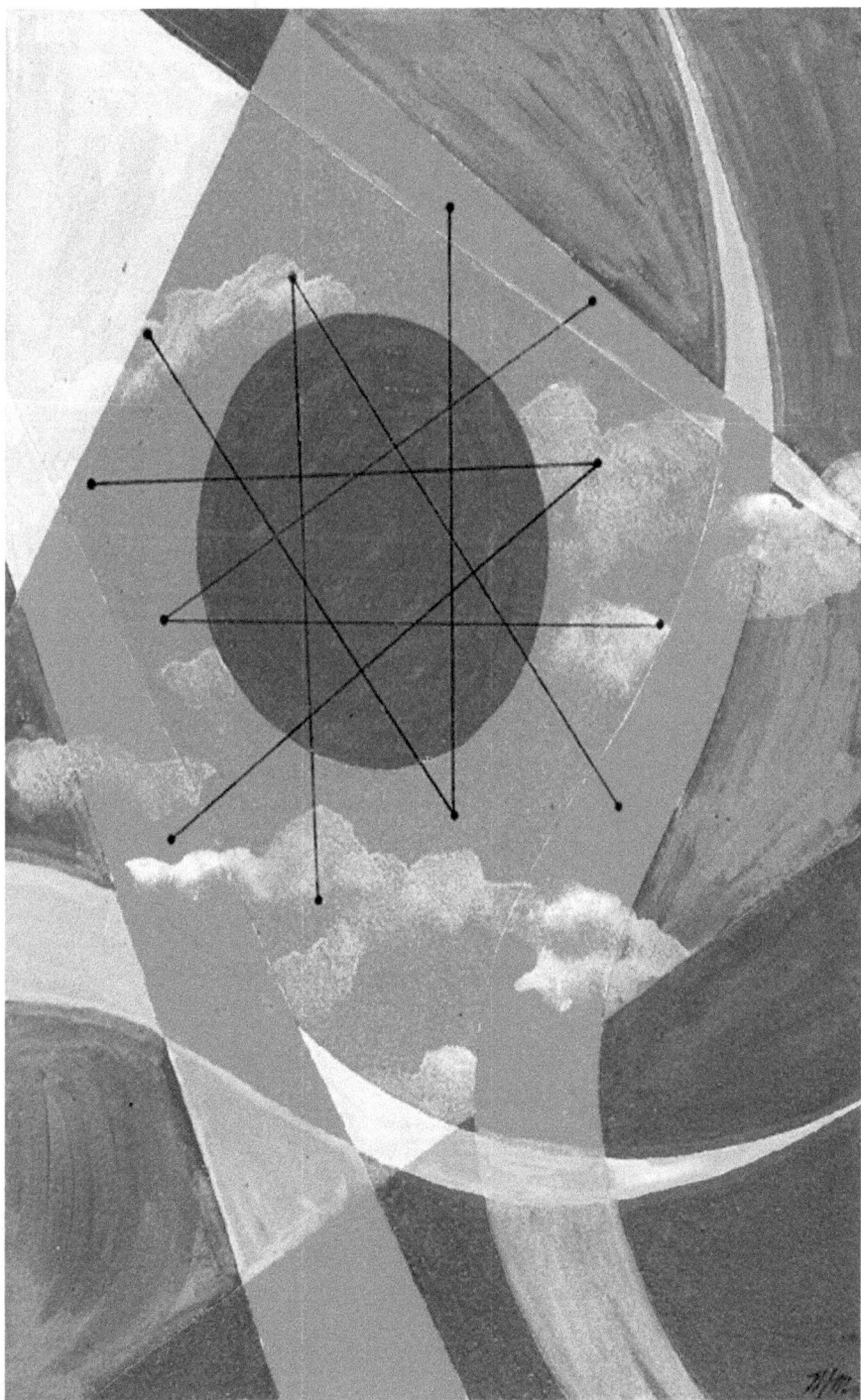

12 and 12 lines

We'd meet every day or so,
Never let on that I was feeling so bad.
How I wanted to let you go,
But I denied all the feelings I had.
You were there when I needed it most,
When I lost the one I loved before.
You knew me better than I myself.
You gave the hope to live for.
You gave me time to get by,
But once again the love is gone.
Now I want to move on, because
You were just another to live on.

I've woken up and I have grown.
Collective sickness is overblown.
Your old ideas are overthrown,
Time marches by your ideas in stone.
There are other ways to be self-known.
Other ways to change your life's tone.
And break free of the dysfunctional zone.
I don't need to pick up the phone,
Or get together to cry and moan.
My past and present is mine to own,
And it's up to God what I am shown.
Other than that I am A.lways A.lone.

Oh Little Town
of Los Angeles

Oh little town of Los Angeles
How fast we see thee grow
Above the highways and the byways
the noisy cars do go.

Yet in the dark streets creeepeth
The ever faithful crook
All his yearnings are for your earnings
that last night he took.

Leave

I yelled
"Leave"

and you turned
You obedient bastard.

I am not your master
don't assume I want
to chain you down
guide the leash.

I am sick of the power play.

And one more thing
before you turn tail,

don't.

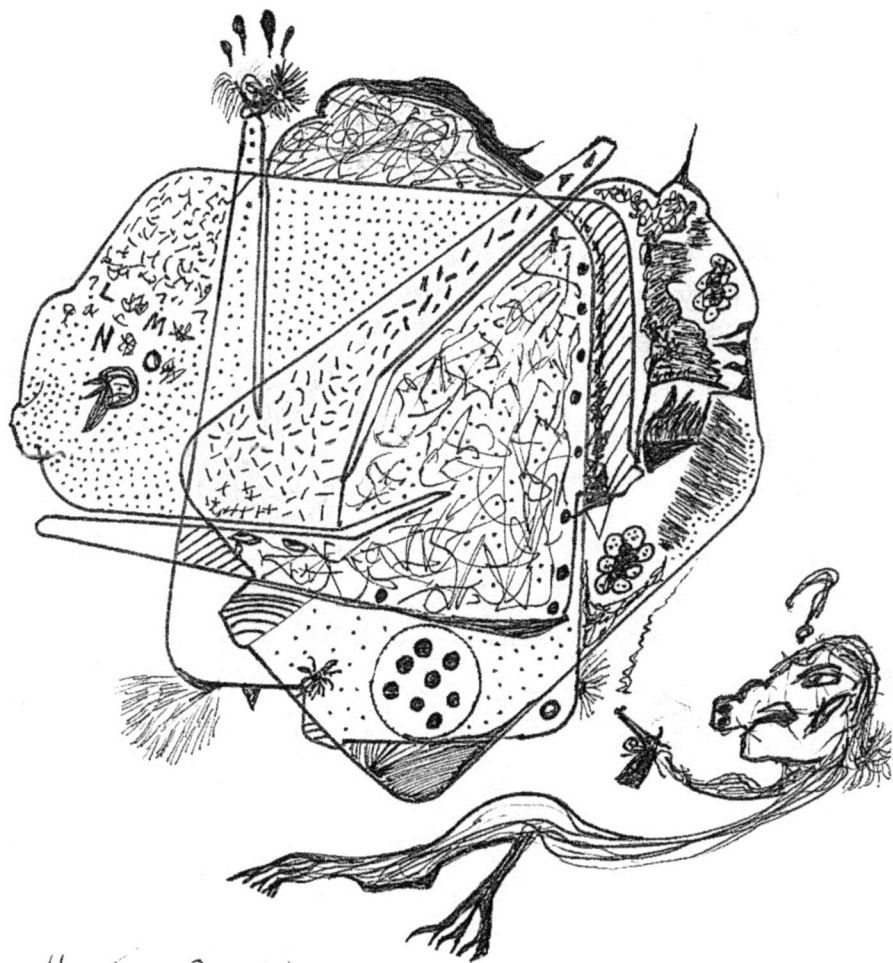

loss

I lean towards you
in a half drunken state
and caress the pillow
that shapes your body.
Tears tumble
as I kiss the pillowslip
and curl my thighs
around another
to squeeze
your absence
away.

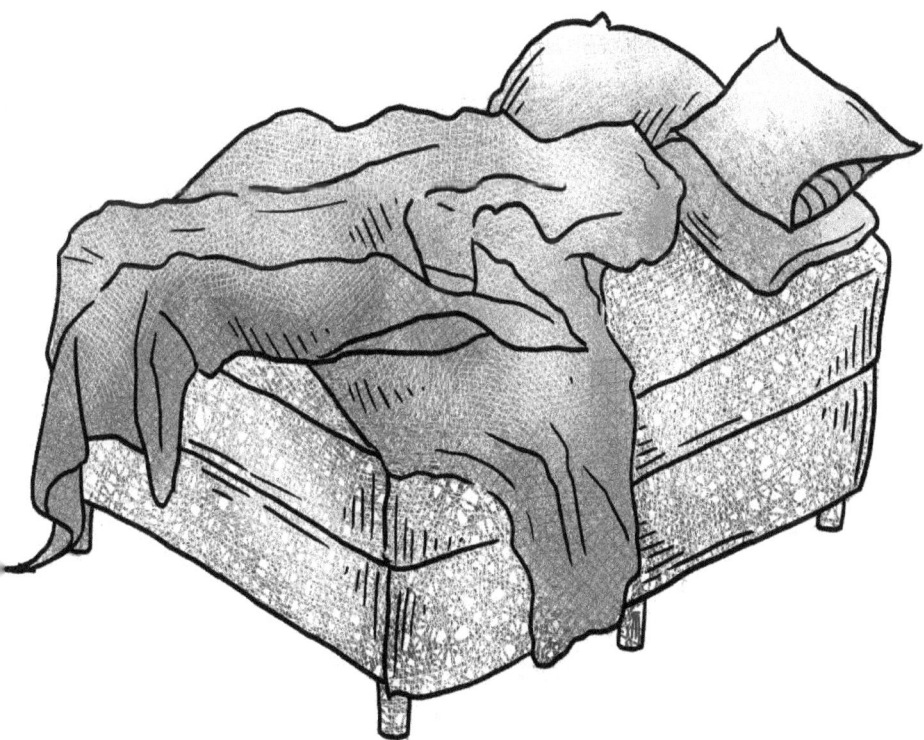

A MidWinter Night's Dream

Lysander, Lysander, how much you knew.
My course of true love never did run smooth.
The wild waters rage, not clear, still, and blue.
Rushing towards death, and running from truth.

Along the way, the murky muck lingers,
Of unfinished business, family conceit,
Dashing hopes with such heart wrenching wringers
On rocks of denial, and deep self-deceit.

How can one steer this white knuckle gripper?
To remain in grace? Remain in the light?
Turbulence tests the well-seasoned skipper,
To remain true, unscathed, and watertight.

Hoping downstream where the river runs wide,
To float in deep peace in a calm ocean tide.

Potomac River 8-16-06

about the author~illustrator

anand has been published
by Westwind - UCLA's
Journal of the Arts,
Manuscript Magazine,
Seventeen Magazine, and
other journals of creative
writing. She enjoys writing
short and punchy,
irreverent and insightful
poetry and prose. By day she is a professional
creative communications consultant. By night,
a musician and artist. She longs to spend a year
in Paris painting, and a year in Manhattan
painting the town.

anandsahaja.com

other works by anand:

Non Fiction

Dominant Health
Eat Like Eve
The Good Wiccan Guides
How Modern Was
   My Valley
Kiss Addiction Goodbye
Kiss Addiction Away
Marry & Grow Happy
Mondo Vegas
Pop Tags – Volumes 1&2
Stop Picking on Me
SPOM Workbook
The SoLa SoFiA Method

Fiction/Prose

Endings?
An Heirloom Adventure
My Life As An Angel
One Toy, Two Toys, Too
   Many Shoo Toys
Please Don't Eat My
   Friends
Sex & Single Girl
   Revisited
Wheel of the Year
Why Am I?

about the illustrators

Bernarda Saldo hails from Croatia. She likes coffee, dogs, South Park, sunsets and bread, in no particular order! She is a trained illustrator and especially loves to work in the black and white mode in both an abstract and literal style. She feels, "There is a special bond between poetry and illustration."

Instagram: crtamito

~ pages 11, 15, 23, 25, 31, 33, 41, 47, 51, 57, 59, 63, 65, 67, 73, 77, 85

additional illustrators

Cary Brian Stratton ~ CBS aka Chef Mason Green is a colorful musical performer and artist CaryStratton.com ~ page 27, 39, 87

Alen Burazerovic is an illustrator with an MFA in printmaking, and a character animator from Bosnia and Herzegovina. Instagram: alenburazerovic ~ pages 43, 48, 54, 69

Angela Li James is a student of architecture in the Central University of Venezuela. Instagram: lili.ael ~ pages 37, 61

Bianca Stancu is a watercolor painter and bird enthusiast from Romania. behance.net/inking_dove ~ 71, 89

Thank you for listening.

www.ingramcontent.com/pod-product-compliance
Lightning Source LLC
Chambersburg PA
CBHW071056040426
42443CB00013B/3356